Story by Story

A JOURNEY INTO THE GOSPELS

WENDI LOU LEE

Cover & interior design by Typewriter Creative Co.
Cover image by Opal Creative on CreativeMarket.com.

Scripture quotations marked (NIV) are taken from the Holy Bible, New International Version®, NIV®. Copyright © 1973, 1978, 1984, 2011 by Biblica, Inc.™ Used by permission of Zondervan. All rights reserved worldwide. www.zondervan.comThe "NIV" and "New International Version" are trademarks registered in the United States Patent and Trademark Office by Biblica, Inc.™

Scripture quotations marked (NLT) are taken from the Holy Bible, New Living Translation, copyright ©1996, 2004, 2015 by Tyndale House Foundation. Used by permission of Tyndale House Publishers, Carol Stream, Illinois 60188. All rights reserved.

Scripture quotations marked (AMPC) are taken from the Amplified Bible, Copyright © 2015 by The Lockman Foundation. Used by permission. lockman.org.

Scripture quotations marked TPT are from The Passion Translation®. Copyright © 2017, 2018, 2020 by Passion & Fire Ministries, Inc. Used by permission. All rights reserved. ThePassionTranslation.com.

Scripture quotations taken from the (NASB®) New American Standard Bible®, Copyright © 1960, 1971, 1977, 1995, 2020 by The Lockman Foundation. Used by permission. All rights reserved. www.lockman.org.

Scripture quotations marked MSG are taken from THE MESSAGE, copyright © 1993, 2002, 2018 by Eugene H. Peterson. Used by permission of NavPress, represented by Tyndale House Publishers. All rights reserved.

ISBN 979-8-9881684-4-7 (Paperback)
ISBN 979-8-9881684-5-4 (eBook)

Contents

Hello and welcome.

I'm so glad you are here.

If you've read my first book, *A Prairie Devotional,* you know all about my Grandma Lou and the famous headless chicken story she told me and my sisters countless times around the dinner table. It always started the same way: "Gram, tell us a story." She'd wave her hand in dismissal. "You girls have heard every one of my stories a dozen times." We'd giggle and plead, "Tell us the chicken story again... please!"

I remember sitting on the edge of my seat, filled with wonder and captivated by every detail, even though at ten years of age I could have recited the entire tale myself. You could say I learned my storytelling skills from Grandma Lou, but the art of storytelling goes back to the beginning of time.

Picture a weathered elder sitting before a crackling fire, the whole village—children, teenagers, and adults—leaning in to catch every word of a story from generations past. Some hearing it for the first time, others preparing to become the next storytellers when the elder's time on earth was over.

The Bible is often called the Word of God in printed form, but long before scrolls and ink, before printing presses and bookstores, the ancient stories of God and His people were passed down through oral tradition—much like my grandmother sharing tales of life on a Minnesota farm around the table. The primary means of preserving everyday happenings, historical accounts, laws, and religious beliefs depended on storytelling around fires and dinner tables.

My children never heard Grandma Lou's stories firsthand, but that's the beauty of oral tradition. Though she'd been gone for years before Tobey and Raegan were born, the honor of sharing her stories passed to me. As soon as they were old enough to handle the thought of a headless chicken running around the farmyard, I delighted them with Grandma Lou's famous tale. And I shared other stories too—like the time our family got stranded in the middle of a lake for hours, rigging up ski ropes to the bow of our boat and kicking our way to shore. A memorable childhood mishap became a lesson in perseverance and working together as a family.

I can't count the number of times I've heard the plea, "Mom, tell us a story," followed by the inevitable stream of curious questions. Story by story, I passed decades of learning and laughter and love on to them. My hope is that one day they will do the same.

There's nothing more inspiring than hearing a real-life story with unexpected twists and turns. These narratives cause us to think critically, make keen observations, and ask probing questions. Bible stories are no different. My favorite chapters of the Bible are the stories of everyday people loving God as they go through life—and that's where you come into the picture.

THE HEART OF THIS STUDY

I'm inviting you to join me in exploring twelve gospel stories, following Jesus from His early ministry through His ascension. Together, we'll listen and learn to make critical observations. We'll rekindle our childlike wonder for Jesus as we ask curious questions about the text and discover how it applies to our lives today. And as we do, our hearts and minds will be transformed. Will you join me as we get to know Jesus, story by story?

WHO THIS STUDY IS FOR

It's for you... and for me. It's for anyone who wants to explore the stories of the Bible with fresh eyes and an open heart. You may have heard these stories a hundred times or never at all. God wants to speak to every one of us through His living Word.

HOW TO USE THIS STUDY GUIDE

This study can be completed individually or in a group. If you choose the group option, I recommend keeping it small—six to eight people maximum—so everyone has an opportunity to share discoveries and insights.

You will need the following materials:

- Bible – any translation or you can use a Bible app on your phone.

- Notecards or sticky notes for our Verse of the Week activities.

- An open heart and mind as I will be asking you to reflect and respond in various ways.

WHAT YOU NEED TO KNOW

We'll be using a **retrospective approach** to Bible study, looking back and revisiting both the stories we have read and the experiences we have lived. We'll use these encounters with Scripture and life to guide us into deeper understanding as we observe what's happening in each narrative.

The **Inductive Study Method** will be our compass as we make observations about each passage, drawing conclusions and making practical application from what we discover. Simply put, I'll be challenging us to dig deeper into Scripture by asking: *Who, What, Where, When, Why,* and *How.*

HOW THIS STUDY WORKS

Every session follows a five-day format, focusing on one specific story of Jesus engaging with everyday people. However, feel free to adapt this to your schedule—whether that means a little each day or settling in for longer study periods once or twice a week. While I recommend giving Jesus your first few minutes each day, you don't have to complete your study time in the morning. Find what works best for you.

As we refocus our minds, read His Word, ask God to reveal His truth, take time to reflect and integrate what we've learned, and then respond with honesty and vulnerability, God will transform these simple stories into storehouses of revelation and application for our lives.

I can't wait to begin this journey with you.

Wendi

The Source

Welcome to our first session together studying the Word of God and letting it take root in our hearts. Jesus has so much to teach us this week about carving out intentional time to sit in our Father's presence. He modeled for us how a real relationship with God works. I hope you are ready to jump in because here we go.

> *"Come near to God and he will come near to you."*
>
> James 4:8 NIV

I want to extend all the grace in the world to you as we talk about the importance of developing a consistent practice of spending time with Jesus. It's called a practice because it takes practice. I want you to know that I have struggled with it as much as anyone. We are in this together, committed to growing in our relationship with God. I'm so glad you are here!

So much love,

Wendi

REFOCUS

If you haven't already, refocus your heart by spending a few minutes with God. Now let's dive into our devotion for the week.

> Devotion = just a fancy word for a story with spiritual insight

I woke up one January morning to the distinct scent of dry pine needles. My not-so-evergreen Nordmann fir stood in the corner of our living room, its glorious green brilliance long faded. The holiday centerpiece had been dropping needles for at least a week, and even the twinkling lights and glass ornaments had lost their allure, hanging from browning branches. Time to strip the decorations and haul the tree outside for the burn pile. Amazing how quickly a cut tree's beauty fades.

My Nordmann had originally grown in the mountains of Oregon, its deep roots soaking up life-giving nutrients from the forest floor. It lived quite happily there, connected to a wellspring of growth opportunities, until the tree cutters felled my gorgeous evergreen. Everything changed in one swing of the axe. Christmas trees may look fabulous for a while, but every cut tree travels a slow journey toward death.

Our dying tree perfectly illustrates what happens when we're severed from our source of life. Trees can't survive it—and neither can we. We need constant connection to the Source if we want a vibrant relationship with Him. Our roots of faith must run deeper than surface level to experience true growth and transformation. When we daily inhale God's grace, peace, and wisdom we gain strength to exhale those same gifts to others around us. Kindness, joy, and generosity don't flow from dead branches—how could they?

This reminds me of an experience my husband and I had in 2015 traveling to New Zealand's famous Milford Sound, where glacier water meets salt water. During our bus ride, the driver pulled over beside a stream flowing with glacier water— "the cleanest, purest water on the planet," he called it. "Straight from the source." We filled our bottles from that stream and tasted the coldest, sweetest water I've ever experienced.

Spiritually speaking, that's exactly what happens when we go to the Source. Our time with Jesus becomes the most refreshing, life-giving experience to quench our weary souls.

So, how do we stay connected to the Source of life? How do we soak up God's constant supply of spiritual nutrients? The answer is simple: spend time with Jesus. Every. Single. Day.

Maintaining a consistent relationship with Jesus sounds manageable, but we all know how life's busyness interferes. Perhaps that's why Jesus rose early, while it was still dark, to find a solitary place with His Father. What if we made the same intentional plan Jesus did? When we deliberately connect ourselves to the Source, we drink in His life-giving comfort, perfect peace, and refreshing grace to guide us through life's journey. And we just might find ourselves reflecting His light more brightly each day.

Let these verses refocus your mind and let the Source of all life speak to you.

- **Psalm 5:3**

- **Hebrews 4:16**

- **1 Chronicles 16:11**

VERSE OF THE WEEK

Write out the verse that spoke to you in the space below.

Now write it again on a notecard or sticky note and place it somewhere you will see it this week. If possible, commit it to memory.

DAY 2: THE SOURCE

READ HIS WORD

Did you start your day with God? If not, go to Him now and surrender this study time to Him.

We are starting with a very short but impactful passage for this first session together. One of the most challenging areas in our spiritual journey is staying connected to God. Let's turn to Mark 1:35-38 to see exactly how Jesus maintained His connection to the Source.

Read Mark 1:35-38

DIG DEEPER

This is where we dig deeper into our passage. Utilizing inductive reasoning, complete at least one of the following study options or more if you have time.

- **Examine the context.** Take a look at the first 34 verses of Mark 1. What's going on?

- **Cross-reference related passages.** Read the story from another gospel (Matthew 4:23-25 or Luke 4:42-44). You could also see what a different translation might reveal.

- **Consider multiple perspectives.** Think about the passage from each character's perspective.

- **Consult a commentary** if you're feeling stumped.

Suggested Commentaries

I have *Jon Courson's Application Commentary*, Volumes 1-3. You can find an online version too.

What stands out to you?

Inductive
Reasoning =
Ask yourself
Who, What,
When,
Where, Why,
and How

DAY 3: THE SOURCE

REVEAL

Go to our passage in Mark 1 and ask God to reveal Himself to you. Look at what you learned in your study time yesterday and make observations while considering the following questions:

- What was Jesus doing just prior to this passage?

- Where else do you suppose His disciples would go looking for Him?

- Why do you think Jesus chose solitude over bringing the disciples with Him?

MAKE OBSERVATIONS

If making observations feels new to you, don't worry—there's no trick to this. Just write down what you read with a bit of curiosity. I will always share my observations with you, in case you're having trouble.

1.

2.

3.

4.

5.

MY OBSERVATIONS

1. It was early in the morning, still dark.

2. Jesus got up on his own and didn't take anyone with Him.

3. Jesus went to a place with no distractions.

4. Jesus must have spent significant time there because the disciples went looking for Him.

5. After his time on the mountain, God directed Jesus to go to another village.

6. Following a busy day of ministry, Jesus sought out a time to get away to be with God.

Did you make some of the same observations? And what did those observations make you think about?

DAY 4: THE SOURCE

REFLECT

This is where we contemplate and apply what we have learned from our passage of Scripture. Start by inviting God into this process. He wants to meet you here.

This first week of our study is centered on spending quality time with God. If He is the Source of life, then we need His presence integrated into our daily routines. We saw in our passage, how Jesus prioritized time with His Father. He models for us what that looked like for Him in the first century. What might it look like for you?

I won't tell you that 5am is the only time you can hang out with God. I'm a bleary-eyed mess at 5am, and thankfully my current schedule doesn't require me to get up that early to spend time with Jesus. The point is to consistently spend time with Him. This could vary in different seasons of your life.

When my children napped, I spent time with God in the afternoon. When they went to school and I worked, I got up early to spend time with God. Your detailed schedule and unique personality will determine when, where, and how you spend time with God.

It's okay to mix it up. Try different approaches to see what works for you or vary your routine each day. The point is to have a plan where consistency can happen.

Take a few minutes to consider your current schedule and circumstances. Now make a plan. If you already have a routine in place... wonderful! Spend this time with God in prayer, meditation, confession or thanksgiving.

Make a Plan	
When will you spend time with God?	
Where will you go?	
What will you do?	
How can you posture your heart to listen?	

DAY 5: THE SOURCE

RESPOND

Every week of study is for the purpose of transformation. I'm praying that God spoke to you this week and you are well on your way to having consistent and sweet times with Jesus.

To wrap up our session, take a look at the following questions. Consider what God might be doing in your heart. Ask Him to show you.

1. In our passage, Jesus recognized his need to be alone with the Father. When are you completely alone with God?

2. In our modern world, we live very distracting lives. How can you protect your time with Jesus by eliminating distractions?

3. What do you have to sacrifice to seek God in the morning (or your chosen time of day)?

4. Who are the people (or things) that might be vying for your attention while you spend time with God? Do you tend to rush through your quiet time to attend to those needs?

PRAYER PROMPT

Focus on one or two of the questions (or more) and write a response to Jesus. Try not to rush this time and enjoy the refreshing waters of His love—the Source of life.

SESSION TWO
Love God. Love People.

Welcome to Week Two of our study.

I am convinced that the best way to start the day is with Jesus. As we surrender our roles and responsibilities into His loving care, He will guide our hearts and minds. Even if it's just five minutes of honest communication on your way to work or while drinking your morning cup of coffee. Remember, you don't have to complete your personal study time in the morning, and the days of this study can be split up however you want to—a little each day or a few larger chunks of time during your week.

> *"I rise early, before the sun is up; I cry out for help and put my hope in your words."*
>
> Psalm 119:147 NLT

Last week, we started with the basics of spending time with God, and we will continue to set the stage by looking at what our Savior was most passionate about.

So much love,

Wendi

REFOCUS

If you haven't already, refocus your heart by spending a few minutes with God. Now let's dive into our devotional for the week.

Back in the '90s, I attended a small Christian college in Southern California. I received a BA in psychology and a minor in Biblical Studies. My psychology courses gave me a deep understanding of the human experience—all from a biblical perspective. What a thrill to experience learning filtered by the words of Jesus. After attending public school my whole life, it felt strange being graded on reading the Bible and writing papers about what God was revealing to me. I'll never forget the class of all classes—Biblical Theology, or Bib Theo as we called it. One lecture, in particular, has stuck with me all these years. In fact, at college reunions with friends, the topic of "Bene and Esse" still takes over our conversations. Here's the gist of it.

When considering biblical theology there are many differing opinions and traditions in the Christian faith. While many of them may be beneficial (bene), not all of them are essential (esse). The unit of study consisted of determining what core beliefs are essential and which are solely tied to a denomination or tradition. This discussion grew quite intense, with many of my fellow classmate challenging our professor on several points.

I remember thinking, *What would Jesus say if he was here? Would he have the same bene/ esse categories as me?* I realized how much I didn't know about God, and now, 25 years later, I still don't know the Father's heart as much as I'd like to. At times, I've let my personal opinions and spiritual upbringing matter more than what Jesus stood for. I've decided to stop trying to figure it out on my own and instead hold tightly to what He said were the greatest of all commandments: Love God and Love People.

I'm committed to anchoring myself to what Jesus called the greatest commandments—they cut through the complexity to what truly matters. When I'm unsure about a theological debate or church practice, I ask: *Does this help me love God more? Does this help me love people better?* These two commands have become my filter for everything else.

Let these verses refocus your mind toward what Jesus values most.

- **John 15:13**

- **1 Corinthians 13:4-7**

- **1 John 4:7-8**

VERSE OF THE WEEK

Write the verse that spoke to you in the space below.

Now write it again on a notecard or sticky note and place it somewhere you will see it this week. If possible, commit it to memory.

DAY 2: LOVE GOD. LOVE PEOPLE.

READ HIS WORD

Did you start your day with God? If not, go to Him now and surrender this study time to Him.

In a world of differing opinions, discerning the heart of God can be a challenge. Even in our Jesus-loving church communities, we get it wrong from time to time. Let's turn to Matthew 22 and discover what Jesus had to say about this. Read verses 34-40.

Read Matthew 22:34-40

DIG DEEPER

Remember the following ways to dig into our passage are just ideas to further your study. You can pick and choose each week depending on how much time you have or complete them all.

- **Examine the context.** Scan verses 15-33 to see the context of our passage. Notice how Jesus has been answering tricky questions from the religious leaders. How do these additional verses inform our reading today?

- **Cross-reference related passages.** Now read the same story in another gospel (Mark 12:28 or Luke 10:25). Or try reading it from a different translation. (The Message and the Passion Translation are two of my favorites.)

- **Consider multiple perspectives.** Think about the passage from each character's viewpoint. Put yourself in the shoes of the religious leaders and the Jewish people listening to this interaction.

- **Consult a commentary** for further insight.

What stands out to you?

DAY 3: LOVE GOD, LOVE PEOPLE.

REVEAL

Go to our passage in Matthew 22 and ask God to reveal Himself to you. Look at what you learned in your study time yesterday. Use your inductive reasoning skills and make observations while considering the following questions:

- What do you notice about Jesus answering the Pharisees?

- What is Jesus saying genuine love for God must include?

- What do you think is the motivation behind the commandments of the Old Testament?

MAKE OBSERVATIONS

Remember, don't make this too tricky. Just write down what you read with a bit of curiosity. My observations are below if you need help.

1.

2.

3.

4.

5.

MY OBSERVATIONS

1. The Pharisees and Sadducees looked for a way to discredit Jesus.

2. Jesus answered quickly—He was prepared.

3. Jesus quoted Moses in Deuteronomy 6:5, He had the verses memorized.

4. Jesus said, if you love God, then loving others flows from that love.

5. Loving God and loving others is used as a guide to follow every other commandment.

Did you make some of the same observations? And what did those observations make you think about? If your observations were completely different than mine, that's great. Way to think outside the box.

DAY 4: LOVE GOD. LOVE PEOPLE.

REFLECT

This is where we contemplate and apply what we have learned from our passage of Scripture. Start by inviting God into this process. He wants to meet you here.

Our second week of study gives us a peek inside the heart of Jesus. He lived His life based on the commandment given to Moses by God in Deuteronomy 6. And then, He transformed its meaning by challenging his audience to apply the same love for God to the people around us. I love how Jesus painted a picture of the cross with His upward love for God and His side-to-side love for others.

Take a few minutes and read Deuteronomy 6. How do these verses from the Old Testament help you understand our passage in Matthew better?

Let's consider how these two commands play out in our daily lives.

1. Why do you love God?

Develop an answer, based on Scripture, that you could use if questioned about the hope you have in Jesus. Focus on the two commandments that Jesus said were essential and let go of the rest as beneficial. Something as simple as "God loves me" with a scripture verse is perfectly complete and acceptable.

2. If we love God, then we will be compelled to love people.

Review your verse of the week about loving others. Think of one person you could demonstrate love for today and brainstorm some possible ideas in the space below. If possible, go do it.

DAY 5: LOVE GOD. LOVE PEOPLE.

RESPOND

Every week of study is for the purpose of growing closer to God and for transformation in our lives. I'm hoping and praying that God's Word has penetrated your heart to align your passions with His.

To wrap up our session, take a look at the following questions. Consider what God might be doing in your heart. Ask Him to show you.

1. If and when someone tests your understanding of Scripture, how will you respond?

2. How have you let your opinions and beliefs about God get in the way of loving God and loving people above all else?

3. Who are the people in your life that are hard to love? How can you demonstrate an act of love to one of these people?

4. Have you ever justified your unloving behavior based on something you read in Scripture? Whose words do you value the most?

PRAYER PROMPT

Focus on one or two of the questions and write a prayer to Jesus. Process your responses with God and see what He might be revealing to you.

SESSION THREE
Go Deeper

You've made it to Week Three. Congrats!

I hope you are loving this study and our time together so far. We have learned about spending time with Jesus and what He called the two greatest commandments. As we dig into another familiar passage, I encourage you to put on your curiosity hat. Focus on what Jesus might be revealing to you about your salvation story as we look at how Jesus called His first disciples. Our conversion stories vary in time and place, but every one of us has a miraculous story of grace. Jesus called Peter to put out his nets in deeper waters. Imagine what could happen when we follow Jesus into the deeper waters of His love.

> *"I pray that from his glorious, unlimited resources he will empower you with inner strength through his Spirit. Then Christ will make his home in your hearts as you trust in him. Your roots will grow down into God's love and keep you strong."*
>
> Ephesians 3:16-17 NLT

So much love,

Wendi

REFOCUS

If you haven't already, refocus your heart by spending a few minutes with God. Now let's dive into this week's devotion.

I've never been much of a fisherman. Most of my fishing memories happened at the lake with my family on our floating barge—think houseboat but without walls. As my sisters and I waited for breakfast and the sun to warm up the water, we would gather on the back deck. The murky reflection, just clear enough to see the bottom, revealed our hopeful catch of six-inch scaly friends. We had no interest in eating them. Fishing was more about filling the empty time than filling our growling stomachs. With a bunch of old poles, a jar of salmon eggs, and the smell of bacon drifting from the open-air kitchen, we dropped our lines. I think my clever mom sold us on the idea so she could cook the morning meal in peace. We'd get a few nibbles, maybe hook one unfortunate bluegill, and then ditch the poles as soon as the breakfast bell rang.

Looking back now, two very important things kept us from catching fish. Deeper water and a deeper commitment. If you and I want to catch big fish—picture-worthy fish—then we have to go to deeper water. Going to deeper water to find a larger catch takes time, dedication, and the necessary gear. Like most lessons in life, what we learn goes with us.

When it comes to fishing and our spiritual lives, intentional positioning and a clarity of focus will always bring about better results. Take a leap into the vast waters of God's love. Dive to the depths and experience all that He has to offer you. Don't just dabble in following Jesus, quitting as soon as the bacon is on the table. Follow Him whole-heartedly, willing to leave everything behind. The deeper we go, the more of God we will catch.

Let these verses refocus your thoughts about going deeper with God.

- **Isaiah 55:6**

- **Proverbs 8:17**

- **Acts 17:27**

VERSE OF THE WEEK

Write out the verse that spoke to you in the space below.

Now write it again on a notecard or sticky note and place it somewhere you will see it this week. If possible, commit it to memory.

READ HIS WORD

Did you start your day with God? If not, go to Him now and surrender this study time to Him.

Going deeper in any endeavor takes hard work and a strong faith to believe the extra effort will make a difference in the future. Let's turn to Luke 5:1-11 and see what Peter experienced when he took to deeper waters.

Read Luke 5:1-11

DIG DEEPER

Remember, the following ways to dig into our passage are just ideas to further your study. Pick and choose which study methods you want to use.

- **Examine the context.** Read the remaining verses in chapter 5 of Luke. How does the concept of going deeper with Jesus continue to be revealed?

- **Cross-reference related passages.** Take a look at another story about Peter fishing in John 21:1-14. Notice how Jesus calls Peter to an even deeper faith.

- **Consider multiple perspectives.** Put yourself in Peter's shoes, pulling up the nets with James and John, the people standing nearby seeing it all play out, and the reaction of Jesus when Peter falls at His feet.

- **Consult a commentary** for additional insight.

What stands out to you?

REVEAL

Go to our passage in Luke 5 and ask God to reveal Himself to you. Look at what you learned in your study time yesterday and make observations while considering the following questions:

- What was Jesus doing when He met Peter?

- How did Jesus involve Peter initially, and then change the course of His life?

- Who did Peter bring along with him?

MAKE OBSERVATIONS

You probably have this figured out by now, but in case you need a little help, just write down what you read with a bit of curiosity. Think outside of the box. I will always share my observations with you and it's fine if yours are different than mine.

1.

2.

3.

4.

5.

MY OBSERVATIONS

1. Jesus saw Peter's empty fishing boat and used it to spread His message.

2. Jesus taught from the boat, while Peter listened from the shore.

3. Jesus told Peter to go back out and fish again, but this time with the promise of a great catch.

4. Jesus told Peter to go to deeper water.

5. Peter called to his friends to help him with the fish.

6. When Peter saw the miracle, he was humbled by his sin.

7. Jesus offered Peter a new occupation, and he left everything to follow Jesus.

Which observations made you think about this passage in a deeper way?

DAY 4: GO DEEPER

REFLECT

This is where we contemplate and apply what we have learned from our passage of Scripture. Start by inviting God into this process. He wants to meet you here.

REFLECTIVE ACTIVITY

Think about when Jesus called you to follow Him. This may be a walk down memory lane: recounting what happened, where you were, and how you felt in the moment. Take your time remembering all the details. Then write down the similarities and differences you experienced compared to Peter. Not all conversion stories involve a miraculous event—it's okay, mine doesn't either.

If you haven't yet made a commitment to follow Jesus, what is stopping you? What questions do you have? Who might be able to help answer your questions?

Close out your study time today with a prayer of thanksgiving to God for the gift of salvation.

Similarities	Differences

DAY 5: GO DEEPER

RESPOND

We've seen Peter's conversion in our passage and paused to think about our own spiritual journeys of following Jesus. I'm hoping and praying God has encouraged you to go deeper in your walk with Him.

To wrap up our session, take a look at the following questions. Consider what God might be doing in your heart, then ask Him to show you how to go deeper.

1. Jesus saw Peter's boat and used it for ministry. What do you have that Jesus can use in furthering His message?

2. Peter called out to James and John to help him with the large catch of fish. Who are the people you can bring along with you?

3. What might you need to leave behind or sacrifice to go deeper with Jesus?

4. What would a deeper commitment to Jesus look like in your life?

PRAYER PROMPT

Focus on one or two of the questions (or more) and write a response to Jesus. Try not to rush this time. Let God speak to you.

SESSION FOUR
The Wilderness

Dear friends, this is our fourth week together.

I feel as though we have come so far already, and I'm praying for your heart to be open to what God has for us in our next session.

Life isn't always easy. There will be various challenges for each of us along our journeys of faith. Times when we will need God's presence and His Word more than anything. If you know anything about my story, then you might remember my favorite verse of Scripture. It has helped me through many difficult seasons of life.

> *"For my determined purpose is that I may know Him. That I may progressively become more deeply and intimately acquainted with Him, perceiving and recognizing and understanding the wonders of His person more strongly and more clearly . . ."*
>
> Philippians 3:10 AMPC

Does this verse describe your heart to know God more?

This week's passage takes us into the wilderness with Jesus being tempted at every turn. Take your time as you work through the personal study days. It's not easy to look at ourselves closely. Be gentle with yourself and know that Jesus is here with you.

So much love,

Wendi

DAY 1: THE WILDERNESS

REFOCUS

If you haven't already, refocus your heart by spending a few minutes with God. As you read our devotion for the week, start to think about your own wilderness seasons.

Waking up from brain surgery in 2015 was "the best day of my life,"* but the next two months became my wilderness. Everything about my health and recovery teetered on the unknown test results at Mayo Clinic. My faith was strong, but Satan worked overtime creating all sorts of doubts and temptations in my mind. I felt more alone during those days than any other time, wandering through a wasteland of emotions. I'd like to tell you that I had Bible verses galore rolling off my lips, sending the Evil One back where he belonged, but that's not how the story unfolded. One verse, looped on repeat, grounded me against the continuous attacks on my mind and heart. It seems one verse was all I could remember after having brain surgery. The verse, Philippians 3:10, helped me navigate the emotional journey through recovery. While it was a difficult experience, I wouldn't trade it for anything.

I've noticed how suffering often follows the most wonderful experiences. We're hit over the head at the sudden reality of it all. God uses our wilderness times to prepare us for the future. It's mind-boggling to realize how God does His best work in us when we are at the lowest, most desperate places. His Spirit moves in and changes us forever. How do we embrace an unknown wilderness? Believing God is in control and that He has a good future ahead of us rests on being saturated in the Word of God. To have truth on the tip of our tongues—even just one verse.

For those of you walking in a present wilderness, remember God is busy shaping and stirring you, making plans for your future, and how He can use you to further His kingdom. Keep

---

* Lee, "Red Tail Feathers", 136.

walking the road Jesus has you on. Be prepared with the weaponry of Scripture, and He will eventually lead you out of the wilderness. And rest assured, you are not fighting the Devil alone. Jesus will help you send him on his way. One verse at a time.

The Word of God can make all the difference when doubts enter our minds. This week, we will be building a collection of verses to arm ourselves for the next wilderness season we encounter. Let's start with these verses and see what encouragement you might receive.

- **Psalm 119:105**

- **Proverbs 30:5**

- **Ephesians 6:16-17**

VERSE OF THE WEEK

Write out the verse that spoke to you in the space below or maybe another verse that has brought you comfort during a hard season.

Now write it again on a notecard or sticky note and place it somewhere you will see it this week. If possible, commit it to memory.

DAY 2: THE WILDERNESS

READ HIS WORD

Did you start your day with God? If not, go to Him now and surrender this study time to Him.

Temptation often lives on the other side of triumph. Jesus endured it in our passage for today, giving us a roadmap to follow. Let's turn to Matthew 4:1-11 and learn how He overcame the devil's taunts.

Read Matthew 4:1-11

DIG DEEPER

Possible ideas for further study of our passage. Pick a few, come up with your own, or complete them all.

- **Examine the context.** Read the last four verses of Matthew 3.

- **Cross-reference related passages.** Look at the story in the gospel of Mark (1:12-13) and Luke (4:1-13).

- **Consider multiple perspectives.** Imagine being in the shoes of Jesus, Satan, and the Spirit who led Him there.

- **Consult a commentary** for additional insight.

What stands out to you?

DAY 3: THE WILDERNESS

REVEAL

Go to our passage in Matthew 4 and ask God to reveal Himself to you. Look at what you learned in your study time yesterday and make observations while considering the following questions:

- What happened right before the Spirit led Jesus into the wilderness?

- What weapon did Jesus use to fight Satan?

- What was the result of the temptation?

MAKE OBSERVATIONS

It's your turn to make observations about our passage. Put your thinking cap on and be curious about what you have read. My observations are below but do this on your own first.

1.

2.

3.

4.

5.

MY OBSERVATIONS

1. Jesus was baptized right before He was led into the wilderness.

2. The Spirit led Jesus into the wilderness.

3. The Tempter came when Jesus was feeling weak from hunger.

4. Satan will always bring God's character into question in a sneaky way.

5. Jesus combatted Satan with Scripture.

6. Satan knows Scripture too.

7. Jesus told Satan to leave, and he did.

What was your most surprising observation from our passage? Does it encourage you to live differently?

DAY 4: THE WILDERNESS

REFLECT

This is where we contemplate and apply what we have learned from our passage of Scripture. Start by inviting God into this process. He wants to meet you here.

REFLECTIVE ACTIVITY

Consider the ways in which Satan has tempted you in the past. He will likely use his same old schemes on you again. Your assignment for today is to identify two or three areas of vulnerability in your internal life, where Satan tends to attack you. This exercise is between you and God and by no means do I want to create any need to hide or feel ashamed. We name these areas with God so He can help us withstand Satan's future attacks more successfully.

For example, my areas of weakness revolve around three major issues: reliving past trauma, loss of purpose, and lack of control. Sometimes these issues, if not dealt with properly, result in panic attacks. Knowing yourself and your areas of weakness is critical to combatting the Enemy. What are your areas of weakness?

Areas of Weakness

Now gather three verses you can use when tempted by the devil. You can use the verses that Jesus used in Matthew 4 or consider doing a Google search. For example: Bible verses for the hopeless, Bible verses for discouragement, Bible verses to fight Satan's attacks. Write down your favorites in the space below and then on an index card so you will be prepared when you need them.

Verse 1

Verse 2

Verse 3

Close out your time with a prayer of gratitude, thanking God for the way He ministers to us through His Word.

DAY 5: THE WILDERNESS

RESPOND

Every week of study is for the purpose of transformation, not just our thinking and habits but our hearts. I'm hoping and praying that God spoke to you about the current temptation or wilderness season you are facing. Times in the wilderness are bound to happen, but God equips us through His Word to not just survive but be transformed. Take a look at the following questions. Consider what God might be doing in your heart. Ask Him to show you.

1. Think of the wilderness seasons in your past. Did they come directly after a time of triumph? And what followed?

2. Have you ever used fasting and prayer to seek God in troubling times? What was the outcome, and if you've never fasted, is it something you are willing to try?

3. We tend to skip over the part that says the Spirit led Jesus into the wilderness to be tempted. Why do you think Jesus needed to be tempted? Why do you think God might have you in the wilderness right now?

4. Jesus told Satan to leave—out loud—and he did. We often give the devil more power than he deserves, acting as if he can read our minds. By the way... he can't. Have you ever told Satan to leave? What do you think about talking directly to Satan?

Focus on one or two of the questions (or more) and write a response to Jesus. It might be about a wilderness season of the past or a current temptation you are dealing with. Jesus wants to walk with you through all your ups and downs. Invite Him to join you on the journey.

SESSION FIVE

Scars

Hey, Friends.

Before we jump into our next week of study, let's look back at our first four sessions and consider what God has been asking us so far.

- Session 1 – Have I been spending time with Jesus every day?

- Session 2 – Is my primary focus loving God and loving people?

- Session 3 – How can I go deeper in my faith?

- Session 4 – What weapons am I using to fight against the temptations of Satan?

Our next five sessions take us along the journey with Jesus from Galilee to Jerusalem.

> *"But forget all that—it's nothing compared to what I am going to do. For I am about to do something new. See, I have already begun! Do you not see it? I will make a pathway through the wilderness. I will create rivers in the dry wasteland.*
>
> Isaiah 43:18-19 NLT

Jesus changes people, and He can change us too. I'm so blessed to be able to share with you today, to tell you that Jesus knows everything about you—your past, your present, and your future.

So much love,

Wendi

REFOCUS

If you haven't already, refocus your heart by spending a few minutes with God. Now let's take a look into at our devotion to introduce our topic for the week.

The sweet strum of a guitar gnawed at my broken spirit. The strings being moved, this way and that, struck a chord in me I can't even begin to describe. I looked around, humbled and in disbelief at my surroundings. *How in the heck did I get here?* Sitting at the kitchen table of music legend, Johnny Cash, I listened to his nephew play a song on Johnny's own guitar. A deep raw melody erupted from this man who looks a lot like Johnny himself. I had only just met him, and yet he willingly shared about the serious battles he had faced over his lifetime and how Jesus had changed him. And continues to change him. I found myself nodding my head in agreement, listening to every lyric with a soul-searching intensity. The battles he had fought again and again produced plenty of scars for my new friend Mark, scars he carries around with him.

I'm convinced we all have plenty of scars. I've often needed just one person to stop and take notice—to sit and listen and nod their head with kindness and understanding to lead me toward a healthier view of myself. That's what Mark Cash did for me. He lined up his scars on that kitchen table and invited me to line up mine right next to his.

Admitting how we've made a mess of our lives is no easy dialogue to begin. It takes courage and a sense of belonging to feel brave enough to let our guards down and share the hardest parts of our stories. I'll never forget the beauty of being in that space and seeing how contagious vulnerability can be.

Sing the lyrics of your deepest regrets. In unison, strum the melody of God's amazing grace over you. It just might change the trajectory of your life. I know it changed mine.

Let the following verses refocus your mind toward grace.

- **Psalm 147:3-4**

- **2 Corinthians 12:9-10**

- **Proverbs 30:5**

VERSE OF THE WEEK

Write out the verse that spoke to you in the space below or maybe another favorite verse.

Now write it again on a notecard or sticky note and place it somewhere you will see it this week. If possible, commit it to memory.

READ HIS WORD

Did you start your day with God? If not, go to Him now and surrender this study time to Him.

We all have regrets over past mistakes. Let's turn to Luke 19:1-10 and see what happened when Jesus met Zacchaeus, the tax collector.

Read Luke 19:1-10

DIG DEEPER

The following are possible ideas for further study of our passage. Pick a few, come up with your own, or complete them all.

- **Examine the context.** The book of Luke follows Jesus on His way to Jerusalem. Flip through the chapters and notice the headings. Maybe jot down the people He engaged with and the parables He told.

- **Explore the uniqueness of this account.** Many of our weekly passages are found in multiple gospel narratives, but not the story of Zacchaeus. What do you think about that?

- **Consider multiple perspectives.** There are many characters in today's passage— Zacchaeus, the crowd, possibly the religious leaders, and Jesus. Consider what each character could have been thinking in the moment.

- **Consult a commentary** if you're feeling stumped.

What stands out from your study time?

DAY 3: SCARS

REVEAL

Go to our passage in Luke 19 and ask God to reveal Himself to you. Look at what you learned in your study time yesterday and make observations, considering the following questions:

- What do you think Zacchaeus's life was like before meeting Jesus?

- How do you think the words and actions of his fellow Jews affected Zacchaeus's view of himself?

- Did Jesus question or judge Zacchaeus in any way?

MAKE OBSERVATIONS

It's your turn to make observations about our passage. Put your thinking cap on and be curious about what you have read. My observations are below—but do this on your own first. See if you are getting the hang of it.

1.

2.

3.

4.

5.

MY OBSERVATIONS

1. Jesus did ministry everywhere He went.

2. Zacchaeus had a controversial occupation in the Jewish community.

3. Zacchaeus didn't know Jesus, but Jesus knew him.

4. Zacchaeus's curiosity prompted him to learn more.

5. Zacchaeus's height prevented him from seeing Jesus, but he found another way.

6. Observers didn't like that Jesus was spending time with Zacchaeus, a sinner.

7. Zacchaeus's employment and socioeconomic status didn't bother Jesus.

Did you make some of the same observations? And what did those observations make you think about?

REFLECT

This is where we contemplate and apply what we have learned from our passage of Scripture. Start by inviting God into this process. He wants to meet you here.

REFLECTIVE ACTIVITY

Imagine being Zacchaeus, up in a tree, about to meet Jesus. What would be going through your head? Draw the series of scenes in your mind, comic strip style, with thought bubbles for both you and Jesus. Take your time with this exercise, even if artistic expression doesn't come naturally to you. (My terrible stick figures would make you laugh.)

Did God reveal anything to you through this exercise?

DAY 5: SCARS

RESPOND

No matter who you are or what regrets you live with, Jesus sees you and loves you. He's willing to forgive your past mistakes and move toward a relationship with you. This week was all about looking inside our hearts to recognize what keeps us from engaging with Jesus.

Consider the following questions and then respond to a few that hit a chord. Don't ignore the prompting of the Spirit—and take your time.

1. How has an interaction with Jesus changed you?

2. Do you believe that Jesus knows all about you and loves you anyway?

3. What parts of your life are you ashamed of?

4. How do you view others who need salvation?

PRAYER PROMPT

Focus on one or two of the questions and write a response to Jesus. Try not to rush this time—let God speak to you.

Be Quiet and Listen

Thanks for coming back for another week of study together. I know you have a million other things you could be doing, but here you are. It makes me so happy I could burst!

Question... have you been finding a few moments to be alone with God each morning? I hope it has been a sweet time that you look forward to each day. If it hasn't worked out so well, remember you don't have to do anything for God to love you. We are not going to be perfect, no matter how hard we try. If you miss a day or a week, or even two weeks, there's no need to get down on yourself. Just pick up where you left off and throw those negative voices in the garbage bin. Living a life of faith is more about *being* with God than *doing* things for God. The *doing* will happen naturally when we focus on the *being* first.

> *"For the source of your pleasure is not in my performance or the sacrifices I might offer to you. The fountain of your pleasure is found in the sacrifice of my shattered heart before you."*
>
> Psalm 51:16-17 TPT

As we continue to open ourselves up to what God has to say in His Word, I am praying for a spirit of surrender to shower down on us. God knows what we struggle with, and He wants us to give Him the space to speak to our hearts.

So much love,

Wendi

REFOCUS

If you haven't already, refocus your heart by spending a few minutes with God. Now let's dive into our topic for the week.

I married one of the world's best listeners. The way my husband leans into a conversation, those big brown eyes focused on every word coming from my mouth is a gift to me and all who know him. He asks all the right questions, causing me to consider new possibilities and helping me communicate my deepest fears and greatest joys. I called him shy after our first interaction (almost 30 years ago), but shy has nothing to do with it. He's a quiet observer on a mission. Listening is his superpower.

If opposites attract, then I'm afraid he got the short end of the conversation. I'm rarely quiet. I would rather talk than listen, giving more advice than asking questions. Heck, I even talk in my sleep. My size 10.5 foot has been rescued from my molars more times than I can count. It's a problem I am intimately aware of and actively working on.

For us talkers, learning to listen can be a challenge. It doesn't feel natural to sit at a quiet dinner table and stay silent for long. I'm finding that growing in my listening skills takes self-awareness and a great deal of practice. Listening is about humility, recognizing that being quiet creates space for others to express themselves, too. It's about noticing how our constant chatter can sometimes drown out God's voice. Listening is being in awe of what God might speak to us in the stillness and waiting in expectation to hear His voice.

I won't ever be a natural listener like my husband, Josh. But just because things don't come easily doesn't mean we give up. To hear God's voice loud and clear, we must practice being quiet and listening to God and others.

Let theses verses encourage you to listen up.

- **Isaiah 28:23**

- **Ezekiel 3:10**

- **Matthew 11:15**

VERSE OF THE WEEK

Write out the verse that spoke to you in the space below or maybe another favorite verse.

Now write it again on a notecard or sticky note and place it somewhere you will see it this week. If possible, commit it to memory.

DAY 2: BE QUIET AND LISTEN

READ HIS WORD

Did you start your day with God? If not, go to Him now and surrender this study time to Him.

As we dig a little deeper into the idea of listening to God, let's look at a story in the Bible. You'll know right away who I identify with in the text. I'm curious to know which character you are most similar to. Turn to Matthew 17 and read verses 1-9.

Read Matthew 17:1-9

DIG DEEPER

Now that you've read this powerful story, let's dig deeper. Here are a few ideas.

- **Examine the context.** Flip back to the section directly before our passage and see what Jesus said would happen.

- **Cross-reference related passages.** Look at the story in the Gospels of Mark and Luke, both in chapter 9. Do you see any differences or insights?

- **Consider multiple perspectives.** What do you think each character was feeling based on their reactions? Jesus, Peter, James, and John. What about Moses and Elijah?

- **Consult a commentary** if you need help.

What did you learn from your study time?

REVEAL

Go to our passage in Matthew 17 and ask God to reveal Himself to you. Look at what you learned in your study time yesterday and make observations while considering the following questions:

- Why do you think Matthew specifically says, "after six days"?

- What do you think makes Peter speak up, while James and John stay quiet?

- How did Jesus model what God announces on the mountaintop?

MAKE OBSERVATIONS

Take time to think deeply about what you have read and make observations. My observations are below if you need help.

1.

2.

3.

4.

5.

MY OBSERVATIONS

1. Jesus only took Peter, James, and John to the mountain.

2. Peter spoke without thinking and wasted no time getting to work.

3. James and John said nothing.

4. Peter recognized Moses and Elijah.

5. The disciples were terrified of God's voice, but not of Jesus.

6. The only words Jesus spoke were words of comfort.

How did your observations differ from mine? And which observation intrigues you the most?

DAY 4: BE QUIET AND LISTEN

REFLECT

This is where we contemplate and apply what we have learned from our passage of Scripture. Start by inviting God into this process. He wants to meet you here.

REFLECTIVE ACTIVITY

If you are a talker like me, then this might be a tough exercise. Pinpoint a time to practice your listening skills with someone in your home. While walking through the neighborhood, driving in the car, or having dinner are all great options. Instead of talking, actively listen to your family member. Look them in the eye and refrain from doing anything else during your conversation. Ask them questions about their day without offering any details about yours. Engage in the conversation for as long as it naturally continues.

Record your experience below.

DAY 5: BE QUIET AND LISTEN

RESPOND

Every week of study is for the purpose of transformation. I'm hoping and praying that God has been speaking to you this week about how to improve your listening skills.

To wrap up our session, ask God to gently bring to mind a time when you regretted speaking up too quickly. Replay the scene in your head and ask yourself the following questions.

1. Why did you speak so quickly, and what happened as a result?

2. Did you miss out on anything while you were talking instead of listening?

3. If you were corrected, how did that make you feel?

4. What did you learn about yourself?

PRAYER PROMPT

Focus on one or two of the questions (or more) and write a prayer response to Jesus. Try not to rush this time, let God speak to you.

Crying Out to God

Friends . . .

I know each of you may be going through something truly hard at this moment. While I don't know the specifics or the duration of your struggles, I do know that God listens when His people cry out to Him.

> *"Then you will call upon Me and come and pray to Me, and I will listen to you. And you will seek Me and find Me when you search for Me with all your heart."*
>
> Jeremiah 29:12-13 NASB

Allow this verse to resonate deeply within you this week. When we seek Him with our entire being, we will find Him with arms open wide. As we cry out to God, the conversation begins, and it is in these moments where a relationship with the one true God becomes more than we ever imagined. God desires to know everything that weighs on your heart—the joys and sorrows, your hopes and dreams, and the most significant challenges of your day. Seek Him and you *will* find Him.

So much love,

Wendi

REFOCUS

If you haven't already, refocus your heart by spending a few minutes with God. Now I'll tell you about a time when I learned to cry out to God in a fresh way.

A year of seemingly unanswered prayers taught me something crucial about how I was communicating with God. I had been offering half-hearted requests—essentially voicing complaints—and unsurprisingly, nothing changed. Month after month, the same pattern continued until I finally recognized the problem: my prayers lacked both humility and confident belief. I had given too much power to circumstances and people, forgetting the One who holds the world in His hands.

Everything changed when I discovered what C.H. Spurgeon meant by "Groanings which cannot be uttered are often prayers which cannot be refused." Sometimes our deepest prayers don't sound like conventional prayers at all—they're more like desperate pleading. Though this might not sound drastically different, the sense of urgent need transformed my prayer practice in a profound way. I began to approach God with deep humility, kneeling in submission, and presenting my requests with unwavering confidence. Immediately, I felt the difference.

I am convinced that God answers prayers in three ways: yes, no, and not yet. While "yes" and "no" are straightforward, the "not yet" answer often feels uncertain. Jesus tells us to pray believing the answer will be "yes" in Mark 11:24. Basically, we are to expect an answered prayer unless He reveals otherwise. So, with renewed confidence, I prayed, supported by a whole group of people, and within weeks, God surprised me with a miraculous "yes."

This led me to consider whether God's "not yet" answers in my life could be due to my own unbelief and lack of humility. The thought of missing out on God's best because of an ineffective prayer life was troubling to me. By aligning our requests with God's will and believing wholeheartedly, we are promised an answer. Although the wait may be long, His "not yet" answers will arrive in His perfect time.

Let these verses refocus our minds on prayer.

- **Mark 11:24**

- **Romans 8:26**

- **James 5:16**

VERSE OF THE WEEK

Write out the verse that spoke to you in the space below or your own favorite prayer verse.

Now write it again on a notecard or sticky note and place it somewhere you will see it this week. If possible, commit it to memory.

DAY 2: CRYING OUT TO GOD

READ HIS WORD

Did you start your day with God? If not, go to Him now and surrender this study time to Him.

As we dive into the topic of prayer, let's see how a blind man cried out to God and received a huge yes. Turn to Luke 18 and read verses 35-43.

Read Luke 18:35-43

DIG DEEPER

Possible ideas for further study. Pick a few or complete them all.

- **Examine the context.** Notice the other stories about prayer in Luke 18. Why might they be grouped together?

- **Cross-reference similar passages.** Three of the gospels have a story of Jesus healing a blind man, or in the case of Matthew, two blind men. Consider the three accounts in Matthew 20, Mark 10, and Luke 18. Note the differences and similarities.

- **Consider multiple perspectives.** Imagine being on the streets of Jericho from each character's perspective: Jesus, the disciples, the crowd, and the blind man.

- **Consult a commentary** for additional insight.

What stands out from your study time?

DAY 3: CRYING OUT TO GOD

REVEAL

Go back to our passage in Luke 18 and ask God to reveal Himself to you. Look at what you learned and make observations by answering the following questions:

- How did the blind beggar ask for help?

- Do you think Jesus knew what the man needed most?

- Why do think it was important for the blind man to voice his specific request?

MAKE OBSERVATIONS

Be curious about what you have read and jot down the facts. Think outside the box if you can. My observations are below, and remember, yours can be different from mine.

1.

2.

3.

4.

5.

MY OBSERVATIONS

1. The blind beggar wasted no time in crying out to Jesus.

2. He humbly asked for mercy.

3. The blind man ignored the crowd telling him to quiet down and yelled even louder.

4. Jesus didn't just pass by; he heard the cries of Bartimaeus and stopped.

5. Jesus asked the man to be specific in his request.

6. Jesus healed his sight based on his belief.

Did you make some of the same observations? And what did those observations make you think about?

DAY 4: CRYING OUT TO GOD

REFLECT

This is where we contemplate and work on what we have learned from our passage of Scripture. I've been praying to God for most of my life, and yet this new terminology of crying out to God has refocused my heart. For me, it seems to be a more expressive and urgent approach to prayer.

REFLECTIVE ACTIVITY

Spend the rest of your study time crying out to God. Bring before Him your deepest requests in humility. Be specific and confident that God is able to grant your request. If you are willing, try a humble posture of prayer. (I like to pray on my knees.)

Record your experience below.

DAY 5: CRYING OUT TO GOD

RESPOND

I've always loved the story of the blind beggar, Bartimaeus. His heartfelt cries to Jesus as he sat by the roadside, and his refusal to quiet down, encourage me to cry out to God with the same spirit. Today, spend your time responding to the following questions and ask God to transform your prayer life.

1. How do the voices around you keep you from crying out to God?

2. Are your prayers general prayers? How might you pray more specifically?

3. Do you believe God stops to hear your prayers? When was the last time you got a yes answer?

4. Have your knees hit the floor lately? What other humble postures could you try?

5. What specific request will you be talking to God about this week?

PRAYER PROMPT

Focus on one or two of the questions (or more) and respond by crying out to God for what is weighing heavily on your heart today. Don't rush this time connecting with your Father.

SESSION EIGHT
Who's With You?

Welcome back after seven wonderful weeks together! We are now over halfway through our journey, and I hope it has been as transformative for you as it has been for me.

I've been praying for your private moments with God. I hope you are learning to discern His voice. Remember, if you don't hear anything at first, it's perfectly okay—just be patient. And if you're still getting accustomed to it, here's some good news: the more time you spend with God, the more natural it will feel. Let the silence calm your spirit and bring you peace. If your thoughts begin to drift, offer them to God and continue to listen.

> *"You will show me the way of life, granting me the joy of your presence and the pleasures of living with you forever."*
>
> Psalm 16:11 NLT

So much love,

Wendi

REFOCUS

If you haven't already, refocus your heart by spending a few minutes with God. Now let's dive into our devotion for the week.

I have a dear friend named Sarah who lives in my town. Like me, she's a wife, a mom, and has an identical twin sister—so we have a lot in common. We've known each other forever and meet up for coffee as often as possible. One of us orders two vanilla lattes (one with oat milk, one regular), while the other secures a pair of comfy chairs in the corner. We catch up on all the latest developments: kids, parents, siblings, work. With so much history between us, honest and vulnerable communication is as easy as consuming a bacon date scone—our favorite sweet pastry to share.

We might offer each other a recommendation or some small parenting advice, but more than anything, it's about listening and learning. It's about encouraging each other when times are tough and praying for the strength to not give up. If someone asked me, "Who's with you?" I'd quickly answer, "Sarah." I know she'd jump at the chance to carry my burdens. When we are together, I sense the spirit of God with us, too, deepening our friendship and uniting us in love. I know Sarah will always have my back, probably holding two vanilla lattes. ☺

Whenever I spend time with Sarah, I'm overwhelmed by God's gift of Christian community. Having Jesus-loving friends walking alongside us multiplies our joy and divides our sorrows. These amazing people encourage us when we want to give up and lift us up to Jesus in prayer. They celebrate with us when our hearts are soaring and pick us up when we are lying in defeat. "Who's with you?" is one of the best questions you can ask yourself.

Let these verses refocus our minds as we study friendship this week.

- **Job 2:11**

- **Proverbs 27:9**

- **Ecclesiastes 4:9-10**

VERSE OF THE WEEK

Write out the verse that spoke to you in the space below.

Now write it on a notecard or sticky note and place it somewhere you will see it this week. If possible, commit it to memory.

READ HIS WORD

Did you start your day with God? If not, go to Him now and surrender this study time to Him.

Friends make our lives a whole lot sweeter, and as we will discover in today's story, friends with strong faith can significantly impact our spiritual journeys too. Their faith has the power to lead to our own healing—how incredible is that! Let's turn to Mark 2:1-12 and see how friendship played a role in one man's ability to roll up his mat and walk.

Read Mark 2:1-12

DIG DEEPER

Possible ideas for further study. Pick a few or complete them all.

- **Examine the context.** Look at the five verses following our passage and notice who Jesus refers to as sick.

- **Cross-reference related passages.** Read this same story in other gospel accounts (Matthew 9 and Luke 5). How do they differ from our focus passage?

- **Consider multiple perspectives.** Think about the passage from each character's viewpoint: the friends, the paralyzed man, Jesus, and the religious leaders. Maybe even the crowd.

- **Consult a commentary** for additional insight.

What stands out to you?

DAY 3: WHO'S WITH YOU?

REVEAL

Go to our passage in Mark 2 and ask God to reveal Himself to you using inductive reasoning. Look at what you learned and make observations by answering the following questions:

- To what lengths were the paralyzed man's friends willing to go to bring him to Jesus?

- Do you think they were confused when Jesus said, "Your sins are forgiven"?

- How do you think the friends reacted when the man jumped up from his mat?

MAKE OBSERVATIONS

Be curious about what you have read, jotting down your observations. Thinking critically can help us see a passage of Scripture from a new perspective. My observations are below, if you need help.

1.

2.

3.

4.

5.

MY OBSERVATIONS

1. The house where Jesus was preaching had reached its capacity.

2. The paralyzed man had four good friends willing to carry him to see Jesus.

3. His friends didn't give up when they couldn't get through the door. They went to the roof.

4. Jesus noticed the great faith of the man's friends.

5. Jesus saw the man's greatest need, granting him both forgiveness and healing of his paralysis.

6. The religious scholars questioned Jesus's authority to forgive sins.

7. The man leapt to his feet, and the crowd shouted praises to God.

How did your observations differ from mine? And which observation intrigues you the most?

REFLECT

Now, let's take a moment to reflect on what we've learned about friendship from our passage of Scripture. Friendships are more than necessary as we go through life, especially in our journeys of faith. The paraplegic man would never have encountered Jesus without the help of his friends. What about your friendships?

REFLECTIVE ACTIVITY

Consider the friendships you've had over the years. Make a list in the box below and contemplate how they've changed. Now draw a star next to the names of your closest friends who share your faith. Reach out to at least two of them this week. Extra points are awarded for coffee dates.

If you find yourself in a season without Jesus-loving friends, pray for God to bring new people into your life. Look around and reach out to someone who loves Jesus. The risk of rejection can be intimidating but take one brave step. New friendships are worth the effort.

If you have friends who don't know Jesus yet, how can you help them encounter Him this week?

DAY 5: WHO'S WITH YOU?

RESPOND

When I think about the moment when four friends removed a roof to lower a man to Jesus, I'm filled with awe. The lengths they went to—driven by their faith and love—are truly remarkable. Take time today to ponder these questions, asking God to bring faith-filled friends into your life and to show you how you can be one to others.

1. What good friends do you have in your life? How do these friendships encourage you in your relationship with Jesus?

2. How far would your friends go to bring you to the feet of Jesus? How far would you go for one of them?

3. Maintaining a friendship takes intentionality and effort. What are you doing to deepen your friendships?

4. Do you ask your friends the deep, hard questions? Are you praying for them on a regular basis?

PRAYER PROMPT

Focus on a few of the questions and respond to Jesus in prayer. Don't rush this time. Let God speak to you.

SESSION NINE

Set Free

Welcome to Week Nine!

I hope your heart swells with joy as you reflect on last week's discussion about friendship and the companions on our faith journey. If you haven't yet made plans for a coffee date or a walk with a friend, be sure to do it this week.

Before we move on, let's take a look at the previous four sessions and consider what God has been revealing to us.

- Session Five – How have my regrets impacted my relationship with Jesus?

- Session Six – How can I become a more intentional listener to God and others?

- Session Seven – How can I transform the way I communicate with God?

- Session Eight – Am I encouraging my friends to follow Jesus in a deeper way?

I'm praying for each of you today, that God would reach down and grab your heart as you work through this session.

> *"For I am confident of this very thing, that He who began a good work among you will complete it by the day of Christ Jesus."*
> Philippians 1:6 NASB

Keep seeking the Lord each day, through prayer and your personal study time. Our spiritual maturity depends on it.

So much love,

Wendi

DAY 1: SET FREE

REFOCUS

If you haven't already, refocus your heart by spending a few minutes with God. Now let's take a look at our devotion for today about how God set me free.

I have a twin sister named Brenda. We complement each other like a Dutch apple pie and ice cream, finishing each other's sentences with the same intonation and expression on our identical faces. Whenever we are together, the room erupts with laughter and smiles, but this wasn't always the case. It took a major health scare for God to reconstruct the internal dialogue I'd been wrestling with for most of my life.

For too many years, I chose to live in Brenda's shadow, unnecessarily competing and striving to be Brenda when God created me to be Wendi. Always striving but never succeeding, I didn't experience my true self-worth until after I woke up from brain surgery in 2015. That moment of complete freedom, yelling "This is the best day of my life," might sound silly to some of you. How could facing a brain tumor shift a lifetime of faulty thinking? More importantly, how could one negative thought about myself turn into a coat of chains to carry around for 28 years?

I don't know if I'll ever truly understand—the evolution of my heavy wardrobe or the shedding of it—but I do know that God set me free. Free from the comparing and striving, free from the not-good-enough feelings that weighed me down and limited my potential ministry to the people around me. He removed my too-heavy jacket by rescuing me from my own faulty thinking.

The Evil One can spawn negative thoughts inside our heads through our own doubts and insecurities. He loops those thoughts on repeat, and before we realize it, we are believing lies instead of truth. Almighty God is the only One who can set us free. He is our Rescuer.

Our Deliverer in times of need. We all need God to set us free from something. What is it for you?

Let these verses refocus our minds on the Rescuer. Memorizing God's truth helps replace the lies we've believed with His promises.

- **Isaiah 43:19**

- **Romans 8:1-2**

- **Galatians 5:1**

VERSE OF THE WEEK

Write out the verse that spoke to you in the space below.

Now write it again on a notecard or sticky note and place it somewhere you will see it this week. If possible, commit it to memory.

DAY 2: SET FREE

READ HIS WORD

Did you start your day with God? If not, go to Him now and surrender this study time to Him.

You may not be dragging around physical chains like the man in our story today, but I imagine you have encountered plenty of lies that worked their way into your heart and trapped you in a cycle of faulty thinking. Let's turn to Luke 8:26-39 and find the secret to being set free.

Read Luke 8:26-39

DIG DEEPER

Possible ideas for further study. Pick a few or complete them all.

- **Examine the context.** Read the entirety of Luke 8 and ponder what the theme might be.

- **Cross-reference related passages.** Look at this same story in Matthew 8 or Mark 5, noting any differences.

- **Consider multiple perspectives.** Ponder the passage from each character's mindset: Jesus, the demons, the man, and the townspeople.

- **Consult a commentary** for additional insight.

What did you learn from your study time?

DAY 3: SET FREE

REVEAL

Go to our passage in Luke 8 and ask God to reveal Himself to you. Look at what you learned in your study time yesterday and make observations while considering the following questions:

- Did you notice what Jesus said in Luke 8:16-18? What do you think Jesus wanted to bring into the light in the Gerasenes region?

- Before stepping foot off the boat, were the disciples experiencing any faulty thinking of their own?

- Did you learn how many men are in a legion? How does it make you feel that Jesus rescued a man from so many demons?

MAKE OBSERVATIONS

Put your thinking cap on and be curious about what you have read. My observations are below if you need help.

1.

2.

3.

4.

5.

MY OBSERVATIONS

1. The demon-possessed man met Jesus and his disciples as they got off the boat.

2. The demons knew who Jesus was and what He was capable of.

3. Jesus demanded the demons to come out, they listened.

4. When the pigs ran down the cliff and died, the herders were afraid.

5. The townspeople appeared more concerned about the dead pigs than the set-free man.

6. The people begged Jesus to leave, and He did.

7. Jesus instructed the man to stay there and tell everyone what God had done.

What was the most surprising observation from our passage? Did it make you think about your own life?

DAY 4: SET FREE

REFLECT

This is where we contemplate and apply what we have learned from our passage of Scripture. Start by inviting God into this process. He wants to meet you here.

When we invite Jesus to be our Savior, He immediately rescues us from Satan's power and breaks the chains of sin. However, learning to live in that freedom—sanctification—is a lifelong process. Just as the demon-possessed man needed Jesus's intervention, we too need His power to break the chains that bind us. Taking an honest inventory of our lives is a crucial part of our spiritual transformation.

REFLECTIVE ACTIVITY

Our modern-day demons often come in the form of addictions and negative thought patterns. Search your heart and write down the lies you have adopted as truth, past and present. Surrender each of them to the Rescuer. We also want to express gratitude for areas where God has already brought freedom. I call them success stories. Write those down as well.

Addictions/Lies/Negative Thought Patterns

Success Stories

DAY 5: SET FREE

RESPOND

Every week of study is for the purpose of transformation. I'm hoping and praying that God spoke to you this week and you are ready and willing to be set free.

To wrap up our session, take a look at the following questions. Consider what God might be doing in your heart. Ask Him to show you.

1. The demon-possessed man was set free by Jesus. Have you ever been set free from something? How did it make you feel?

2. In our passage, the demons believed Jesus was real and knew He was the Son of God. Is believing like the demons enough to save you?

3. In our material and idol-addicted world, do you ever prioritize your business investments or hobbies over being in the presence of God?

4. When have you unconsciously asked Jesus to go away by your indifference?

5. Where has God called you to share your testimony of freedom?

PRAYER PROMPT

Focus on one or two of the questions (or more) and write a response to Jesus. Try not to rush this time with God. He wants to speak to you specifically.

SESSION TEN

A Very Dirty Job

You're back!

I'm glad to see you here. For our last three weeks together, we'll explore how Jesus models service, sacrifice, and wonder. We have front-row seats to learn from the greatest example who ever walked this earth.

> *"Watch what God does, and then you do it, like children who learn proper behavior from their parents. Mostly what God does is love you. Keep company with him and learn a life of love. Observe how Christ loved us. His love was not cautious but extravagant. He didn't love in order to get something from us but to give everything of himself to us. Love like that."*
>
> Ephesians 5:1-2 MSG

Ready. Get set. Let's serve.

So much love,

Wendi

DAY I: A VERY DIRTY JOB

REFOCUS

If you haven't already, refocus your heart by spending a few minutes with God. Now let's dive into our devotion for the week.

Davíd knocked loudly at the weathered front door, his arms balancing three Styrofoam containers. "¿Hola, Mariana . . . está usted en la casa?" My friend Megan and I stood behind him with our young daughters, who surveyed the unfamiliar surroundings with wide eyes.

This house didn't share the bright blues and pinks we'd passed along the way. It seemed forgotten—dingy off-white stucco marked with graffiti, windows barred against the world. A torn garbage bag littered the walkway with dozens of food containers. Ants marched in formation while yellow jackets buzzed overhead. The stench hit me like a wall, and I immediately regretted volunteering.

We heard shuffling approach the door. Step, step—drag. Step, step—drag. My eight-year-old clutched her bucket of cleaning supplies, eyes wider than I'd ever seen on her sweet face.

When the door opened, Davíd rushed to help the frail woman settle into her chair, positioning her aluminum walker within reach. He placed the food on the cluttered counter, moving empty containers to make space. A reddish-brown trail had solidified between the refrigerator and the overflowing sink. Remains of refried beans, Spanish rice, and scrambled eggs—along with other unrecognizable leftovers—covered every surface. Our shoes stuck to the floor as we stared in shock.

Davíd sighed. "This is a very dirty job, but Mariana is so grateful for your help. I'll pick you up in two hours. Muchas gracias." He handed Mariana a box of food and a plastic fork, placed his hand gently on her head, prayed quickly in Spanish, and was gone.

My definition of "messy" changed that day. I'll never forget scrubbing Mariana's kitchen, mopping her floors, or hauling four bags of trash away. None of us enjoyed the cleaning, but Mariana's toothless smile and dancing eyes made every moment worthwhile.

Serving Mariana shifted my perspective on what Jesus called "the least of these." Anyone could end up in her situation—alone, without family support or resources. It broke my heart and opened my eyes to the marginalized, both in neighboring countries and right down the street.

The practical side of service is often messy work without recognition. Yet the internal rewards last a lifetime. When I think of Jesus cleaning up my messes, it compels me to serve others. One sticky floor at a time.

Let these verses refocus your mind on serving others:

- **Mark 10:45**

- **Romans 12:10**

- **Hebrews 6:10**

VERSE OF THE WEEK

Write out the verse that spoke to you in the space below.

Write your chosen verse on a notecard or sticky note and place it where you will see it daily. If possible, commit it to memory.

DAY 2: A VERY DIRTY JOB

READ HIS WORD

Did you start your day with God? If not, go to Him now and surrender this study time to Him.

As we explore Scripture about the heart behind serving others, notice how Jesus didn't pick and choose whom He served. Service isn't about who deserves it—we're all needy in God's sight. Let's turn to John 13:1-17.

Read John 13:1-17

DIG DEEPER

Choose a few options or complete them all:

- **Examine the context.** Read the continued conversation around the table (John 13:18-17:26). What kind of guidance does He give?

- **Cross-reference related passages.** Compare other accounts of the Last Supper (Matthew 26:17-30, Mark 14:12-26, and Luke 22:7-23).

- **Consider multiple perspectives.** Step into the shoes of each character of the story: Jesus (knowing what's coming), Peter, and even Judas.

- **Consult a commentary** for additional insight.

What stands out to you?

DAY 3: A VERY DIRTY JOB

REVEAL

Return to John 13 and ask God to reveal Himself to you.

Building on yesterday's reading, consider the following questions as you make observations using the inductive method of reasoning (Who, What, Where, When, Why, and How).

- Are you surprised that Jesus took on the duties of a servant?

- What do think the towel around Jesus's waist looked like after washing twenty-four grimy feet?

- Imagine Judas and what he was feeling as Jesus washed his feet.

YOUR OBSERVATIONS

Be curious about what you've read. Think critically to see this passage with fresh eyes. My observations are below if you need help.

1.

2.

3.

4.

5.

MY OBSERVATIONS

1. Jesus knew His time with the disciples was short.

2. Jesus knowingly washed His betrayer's feet.

3. The Master humbly dressed and served like a household servant.

4. The disciples didn't fully grasp Jesus's meaning of "clean."

5. Jesus could see into the hearts of His disciples.

6. Jesus modeled how godly leaders serve their followers.

7. Jesus instructed His disciples to serve one another.

What was the most surprising observation? Does it challenge you to live differently?

DAY 4: A VERY DIRTY JOB

REFLECT

This is where we contemplate and apply Scripture to our lives. Start by inviting God into this process—He wants to meet you here.

REFLECTIVE ACTIVITY

Think about the people you've served in the past. What did you do and how messy did it get? Remember, some service is emotional or spiritual in nature—your hands might stay clean, but your heart carries the weight.

Who did you serve?	
What did you do?	
Physical or Emotional?	
How challenging was it?	

Now brainstorm a few future service opportunities:

DAY 5: A VERY DIRTY JOB

RESPOND

Every week of study aims for transformation. I'm praying God spoke to you this week and you're thinking about service in a new way.

To wrap up our session, consider these questions and ask God to show you what He's doing in your heart:

1. Do you feel urgency to make a difference in this world? How will you respond?

2. What are your thoughts about serving people who may not "deserve" it?

3. How messy are you willing to get serving others?

4. Many acts of service involve physical cleaning: scrubbing floors, raking leaves, washing a car. Have you considered serving others emotionally or spiritually?

5. Jesus spent His last free evening serving His disciples. What do you want your last days or moments of influence to look like?

Focus on one or two of the questions and write a response to Jesus. Try not to rush this time, let God speak to you.

SESSION ELEVEN
A Future with Jesus

Welcome to another session of studying God's Word together. It's a true blessing to walk alongside you, exploring some of my favorite gospel stories. Our journey wouldn't be complete without visiting the place where Jesus willingly sacrificed His life to save us from our sins. Many witnessed this moment, each with their own reactions. Today's story challenges us to reflect on how we will respond to Jesus's sacrifice. Will we turn away in disbelief, or will we surrender our futures to Him with faith and gratitude?

> *"This is how God showed his love among us: He sent his one and only Son into the world that we might live through him. This is love: not that we loved God, but that he loved us and sent his Son as an atoning sacrifice for our sins."*
>
> 1 John 4:9-10 NIV

So much love,

Wendi

REFOCUS

If you haven't already, refocus your heart by spending a few minutes with God. Now let's look at our devotion for the week.

I grew up attending church, but it wasn't until the summer before high school that my personal relationship with Jesus truly began. As I sat in the chapel at Hume Lake Christian Camp, tears streaming down my face, the decision to follow Christ weighed heavily on my heart. I didn't need to be convinced of God's existence—my belief was strong. The issue rested on going home to my non-believing friends and how they might react. I pictured them mocking my new beliefs and me struggling to articulate what I had just come to understand. At that moment, the fear of stepping into the unknown with God felt overwhelming.

As I wrestled with this decision, I couldn't help but think about Jesus Himself. He knew exactly what awaited Him—the cross, mockery, and being abandonment by those He loved. Yet He chose to move forward anyway, not for His own sake, but for mine. For ours. While I feared the rejection of a few teenage friends, Jesus willingly walked toward the rejection of the entire world.

Thankfully, I chose to take a leap of faith and embrace God wholeheartedly. The initial journey wasn't easy, navigating the complexities of adolescence while saying goodbye to my old way of life. Some of my friends did question my choices, and I suspect a few mocked me behind my back. However, over time, those friendships faded, and new friendships formed with those who also shared a love for God. My overwhelming fears soon diminished, transforming my perspective and becoming a testament to the power of faith.

The mocking I feared paled in comparison to what Jesus endured at Calvary. He faced the jeers of religious leaders, the cruelty of soldiers, and the scorn of criminals—all while bearing the weight of humanity's sin. Yet in His darkest hour, He thought not of Himself but of us, praying, "Father, forgive them, for they do not know what they are doing."*

Like my teenage self, we all face moments when following Jesus requires us to step into the unknown. Rejection, misunderstanding, or standing alone are real fears, but as we look to the cross, we can see how Jesus walked through the ultimate rejection so we might walk confidently into His arms. When those moments of decision come, the peace of God provides the anchor we need to strengthen our resolve to follow Him. No matter the cost.

Let these verses refocus your heart towards our Savior:

- **Isaiah 43:19**

- **Romans 8:1-2**

- **Galatians 5:1**

VERSE OF THE WEEK

Write out the verse that spoke to you in the space below.

Write your chosen verse on a notecard or sticky note and place it where you will see it this week. If possible, commit it to memory.

---

* Luke 23:34

DAY 2: A FUTURE WITH JESUS

READ HIS WORD

Did you start your day with God? If not, go to Him now and surrender this study time to Him.

Jesus not only endured the cross but also the mocking of the people He came to save. Let's turn to Luke 23:32-47 and see how Jesus responded.

Read Luke 23:26-47

DIG DEEPER

I challenge you to complete as many of these study options as possible. Remember to use your inductive reasoning skills as you study.

- **Examine the context.** Read chapter 23 in its entirety, noting those who mocked Jesus and those who embraced Him.

- **Cross-reference related passages.** Take a look at the different crucifixion accounts (Matthew 27, Mark 15, John 19).

- **Consider multiple perspectives.** Ponder the passage from each character's viewpoint—Jesus, the women, the soldiers, the religious leaders, and the two criminals.

- **Consult a commentary** for additional insight.

What stands out to you?

REVEAL

Revisit our passage in Luke 23 and ask God to reveal Himself to you. Look at what you learned in your study time yesterday, and consider the following questions as you make observations:

- Have you ever researched the act of crucifixion and what exactly takes place? If not, I encourage you to do that before you go on.

- Earlier in chapter 23, what was Pilate's role in the crucifixion? What do you see in our passage that demonstrates the effect Jesus had on Pilate?

- How did Jesus respond to the criminal's confession?

MAKE OBSERVATIONS

You've developed strong observation skills through our journey together. Now let's apply them to this pivotal moment in history. As always, my observations are below.

1.

2.

3.

4.

5.

MY OBSERVATIONS

1. Jesus hung on a cross between two criminals.

2. Even while undergoing intense pain, Jesus asked God to forgive those nailing him to the cross.

3. The religious leaders, soldiers, and even one of the criminals sneered and mocked Jesus.

4. The inscription above Jesus's head was written in Greek, Latin, and Aramaic.

5. The only thing the repentant criminal did was confess his sin and humbly ask for Jesus to remember him.

6. Jesus gladly granted the repentant criminal's request.

7. If Jesus had saved Himself, then He wouldn't have been able to save us.

How did your observations differ from mine? And which observation intrigues you the most?

REFLECT

This is where we contemplate and do something in response to our passage of Scripture.

Sometimes we may overlook the profound significance of Jesus's death. The crucifixes in our churches don't fully convey the depth of the event. It can be both helpful and unsettling to imagine ourselves in the crowd, witnessing the crucifixion.

REFLECTIVE ACTIVITY

Take a few moments to imagine being there, watching the whole story play out. What do you think you would see, hear, taste, touch, and smell? Brainstorm in the chart on the following page.

To truly appreciate the sacrifice Jesus made, consider watching one of these impactful films this week:

The Last Temptation of Christ (1988)
The Passion of the Christ (2004)
Risen (2016)

Note: These films contain graphic depictions of crucifixion that may be difficult to watch. Use discretion with young or sensitive people in your home.

See	
Hear	
Taste	
Touch	
Smell	

DAY 5: A FUTURE WITH JESUS

RESPOND

Take some time to consider the following questions, asking God to help you respond with complete honesty. Jesus wants to spend time with you as you think about the sacrifice He made for you.

1. Have you ever suffered unjustly? How did it make you feel? How do you think Jesus felt bearing the sins of the world?

2. When you are in pain, either physically or emotionally, how easy is it for you to forgive those who are hurting you?

3. Have you ever had the chance to stand up for Jesus amid a mocking crowd? How did it play out?

4. Jesus wasn't concerned with the past sins of the criminal asking to be remembered in heaven. Do you think Jesus cares what you've done in the past?

5. What is the only requirement to being saved?

PRAYER PROMPT

Focus on one or two of the questions (or more) and write a response to Jesus. Try not to rush this time, let God speak to you.

SESSION TWELVE
The Hunt for Jesus

Hello, my dear friends.

It brings me great joy to have journeyed through the gospels with you. As we reach the final week, we reflect on following Jesus from His baptism to the cross. Yet, our journey isn't over. We have one last story to explore before we conclude this wonderful study together. It has been such a pleasure, thank you for joining me!

> *"I pray that the Father of glory, the God of our Lord Jesus Christ, would impart to you the riches of the Spirit of wisdom and the Spirit of revelation to know him through your deepening intimacy with him."*
>
> Ephesians 1:17 TPT

So much love,

Wendi

DAY 1: THE HUNT FOR JESUS

REFOCUS

If you haven't already, refocus your heart by spending a few minutes with God. Now let's take a look at our devotion for the week.

When my children were young, they absolutely loved scavenger hunts. I would come up with a variety of fun, rhyming clues that led them on a thrilling quest to uncover a special surprise—whether it was their birthday presents, an Easter basket, or a "Welcome to Summer" bundle of goodies. No matter the occasion, the hunt for clues extended the joy and taught my kids to think critically and observe the wonders around them.

One Easter weekend, I decided to elevate our traditional scavenger hunt by incorporating it into our camping trip in the majestic Redwood Forest near Santa Cruz, California. As my daughter slept peacefully, I quietly tiptoed out of our tent and began hiding clues inside colorful plastic eggs scattered throughout the campground. Given the significance of Resurrection Sunday, I carefully matched each clue with a Bible verse about Jesus. While I can't remember every detail, I do recall placing a yellow egg with the verse from John 8:12 inside, "I am the light of the world," leading to a lamppost, and a blue egg containing the verse from John 4:14, "Whoever drinks of the water that I will give him will never be thirsty again," leading to the water faucet. The grand finale featured an empty egg symbolizing the empty tomb, which led to a basket filled with delicious foil-wrapped chocolate treats.

Our spiritual journeys with God mirror this kind of sacred scavenger hunt. He leaves signs of His unwavering love all around us, hoping we will recognize His presence. Sometimes, the evidence of Jesus is right in front of us, while other times we need to search more diligently to uncover it. The journey to discover His goodness and grace can be challenging, as not every hunt concludes with a basket of sweet treats. Often, grace shows up in the most difficult moments of life, providing us much-needed hope and a reminder that God has not forgotten us.

Just as my daughter had to pay attention to her surroundings to find each hidden treasure, we must cultivate spiritual awareness to recognize Jesus in our daily lives. The greatest treasure of life is a relationship with the Living God. This week, we'll discover how two disciples experienced their own divine scavenger hunt on a dusty road to Emmaus, walking alongside Jesus without even knowing it. Open the eyes to your heart, and let's go find Him.

Let these verses refocus your mind toward the mystery of Jesus.

- **Matthew 13:13-15**

- **Romans 16:25-27**

- **1 Corinthians 2:7-8**

VERSE OF THE WEEK

Write the verse that spoke to you or another favorite verse.

Now write it again on a notecard or sticky note and place it somewhere you will see it this week. If possible, commit it to memory.

READ HIS WORD

Did you start your day with God? If not, go to Him now and surrender this study time to Him.

We will be spending our last week together studying one of my all-time favorite passages. If you have read my memoir, *Red Tail Feathers*, you know I'm always on the lookout to find God's grace around me. Sometimes we can't see Jesus until He's staring us in the face.

Read Luke 24:13-43.

DIG DEEPER

For our last week of study, I challenge you to complete as many of these options as possible:

- **Examine the context.** Read Luke 24:1-12 and Luke 24:44-53. How does studying what happened directly before and after our passage strengthen your understanding?

- **Explore the uniqueness of this account.** Our story is only found in the gospel of Luke. Use your research skills to discover possible reasons why this story wasn't written about in the other gospels. Consider Luke's emphasis on Jesus's compassion for ordinary people and his detailed resurrection accounts.

- **Consider multiple perspectives.** Think about the passage from each character's viewpoint: Jesus, Cleopas (likely a disciple, though not one of the twelve), and his unnamed companion. What might each of them have been thinking and feeling?

- **Cross-reference related passages.** Look at John 20:19-29 and Mark 16:12-13 for additional accounts of Jesus's appearances after the resurrection.

- **Consult a commentary** if you're feeling stumped.

What stands out to you?

DAY 3: THE HUNT FOR JESUS

REVEAL

Go to our passage in Luke 24 and ask God to reveal Himself to you. Look at what you learned in your study time yesterday and make observations while considering the following questions:

- Why do you think Jesus kept His identity hidden from the two disciples on the road?

- What do you think your reaction would have been to a stranger explaining the Scriptures about the Messiah?

- How do you think the disciples felt when Jesus disappeared after breaking the bread?

MAKE OBSERVATIONS

You've developed strong observation skills throughout our journey together. Now apply them to our passage. If you need help, my observations are below.

1.

2.

3.

4.

5.

MY OBSERVATIONS

1. On the day of His resurrection, two disciples—Cleopas and an unnamed companion, not among the twelve—set off from Jerusalem to Emmaus, a journey of about seven miles.

2. Jesus walked alongside them, engaging in conversation, but kept His identity hidden.

3. Jesus sparked the conversation with genuine curiosity, inviting the disciples to discuss recent events and share their confusion and disappointment.

4. Jesus demonstrated His identity as the Messiah through systematic Scripture exposition, explaining how the Law, Prophets, and Writings pointed to Him, yet still they did not recognize Him.

5. Jesus showed perfect respect for their freedom—He didn't force himself on the travelers when they reached the village but gave the impression he was going farther.

6. The moment Jesus broke bread and blessed it—a familiar gesture they must have witnessed before—their eyes were opened, and immediately He vanished from their sight.

7. Despite the late hour and their weariness, they rushed back to Jerusalem to share their extraordinary experience with the other disciples.

How did your observations differ from mine? And which observation intrigues you the most?

DAY 4: THE HUNT FOR JESUS

REFLECT

This time is for you to reflect and integrate the lessons from our Scripture passage. Begin by inviting God into this sacred space. He desires to meet you here.

REFLECTIVE ACTIVITY

Today, embark on your own scavenger hunt to find Jesus. Choose a peaceful spot—perhaps a walking trail, a beach, or a tranquil park. Bring along a bag to collect your treasures and perhaps some water to stay hydrated. As you stroll, be attentive to the signs of God's presence around you. It could be anything: a uniquely shaped leaf, a feather, a smooth stone, wildflowers pushing through concrete, or the last golden rays of sunlight breaking through the clouds.

As you collect each item, pause and ask yourself: *How might this reflect God's character? What does this teach me about His creativity, provision, or faithfulness?* Take a moment to thank God for what you have discovered and for giving you the spiritual eyes to see Him in the ordinary moments of your day.

Record your experience below.

DAY 5: THE HUNT FOR JESUS

RESPOND

Each week of study is designed to bring about transformation. My hope and prayer throughout this study is that you have heard from God in a fresh way and are seeking Jesus in every aspect of your life.

To wrap up our session, look at the following questions. Consider what God might be doing in your heart. Ask Him to show you.

1. Like the two disciples, have you ever been confused by Jesus and feeling alone only to find Him walking right beside you?

2. How has Jesus surprised you with His presence during a difficult season?

3. Jesus won't ever force Himself on you. How does His respectful approach to relationship challenge or comfort you?

4. When has Jesus kept His identity somewhat hidden from you, only to reveal Himself in an unexpected moment?

5. How has an encounter with Jesus encouraged you to "return to Jerusalem" and share your story with others?

6. Does the Road to Emmaus narrative challenge you to be more attentive to Christ's presence in Scripture study, in ordinary conversations, and around your table?

7. What "bread-breaking" moments in your life have revealed Jesus most clearly to you?

Focus on one or two of the questions and write a response to Jesus. Consider how the disciples' hearts "burned within them" as Jesus explained the Scriptures. Ask Him to kindle that same fire in your heart.

Congratulations!

We have completed a twelve-week study exploring Jesus in the gospels. I hope and pray that you have seen growth in your own life. Let's take a few moments to review our last four sessions together. How do you sense God challenging you to embrace Him more fully?

- Session Nine – What have I been set free from? Who can I share my experience with?

- Session Ten – Who am I currently serving? Who else could benefit from my help?

- Session Eleven – What am I sacrificing to live my life for Jesus?

- Session Twelve – How have I seen Jesus in my daily life this week?

In Closing

I've loved developing this interactive devotional for you. Who knows... there may be more interactive devotionals in the future, but until then, you can continue studying the Bible on your own using this same format.

Like those two disciples who couldn't contain their joy after encountering the risen Christ, may you carry the treasure of what you've discovered into every ordinary moment of your life. Jesus is still walking the roads of our daily experience, waiting to be recognized, ready to explain the Scriptures, and hoping we'll invite Him to stay.

WHERE TO GO FROM HERE?

You may be wondering what to do next. I challenge you to apply this method of inductive Bible study to any passage of Scripture. I have included an outline for you to use. Remember, when we utilize a retrospective approach to study familiar Bible stories, they come alive in a fresh way.

OUTLINE FOR FUTURE USE

Refocus – Part 1

• Surrender your time to God, asking Him to direct you in your study time.

Read His Word

Find a story in the Bible you want to learn more about and dig deeper using the study tools we used in each session's Day 2 workbook pages.

• Read the passage in the context of the chapter or book (if necessary).

- Look at the story in another gospel or cross-reference the passage to learn more.

- Read the passage in a different translation.

- Consider the passage from each character's perspective.

- Research historical and cultural context.

- Consult a commentary if you're feeling stumped.

Reveal

- Ask yourself a few questions that crossed your mind during your study time.

- Make detailed observations.

Reflect

- Think of an activity or exercise you can do to experience the passage more fully.

Respond

- Think critically about each of your observations and then come up with 3-5 application questions to ask yourself. Respond to God in prayer.

Refocus – Part 2

- Now that you have studied this passage extensively, consider writing a correlating reflective story from your life. Not only does it cement what you have learned, it also serves as a healthy technique in processing past experiences and recognizing God's faithfulness in your own journey.

Let's Stay Connected

I hope this isn't goodbye. Please share with me how this study challenged and changed you into someone who looks more like Jesus. And if you have a prayer request, I'd love to cry out to God on your behalf. Send me a message through my website's Connect page (wendiloulee.com). It's been an absolute pleasure. Hope to connect with you soon!

Grace + Peace,

Wendi

Great experiences ARE EVEN BETTER WHEN THEY ARE SHARED.

How to help others find this interactive devotional:

- Post a review at your favorite online bookseller.

- Post a picture on your social media account and share why you enjoyed it.

- Tell a friend about it—or, better yet, gift them a copy.

- For orders of ten or more books, please visit Wendi's website to inquire about group pricing.

About the Author

WENDI LOU LEE is best known for playing Baby Grace Ingalls on Little House on the Prairie. Wendi's life took a transformative turn after being diagnosed with a brain tumor in 2015. Her recovery experience, along with a deep love for Jesus, redirected her life's purpose. Sharing the goodness of God through writing and meeting people face to face brings Wendi the most joy. Wendi lives in Pennsylvania with her husband Josh and their Bernedoodle Mo.

Wendi's Other Books

AVAILABLE WHEREVER BOOKS ARE SOLD.

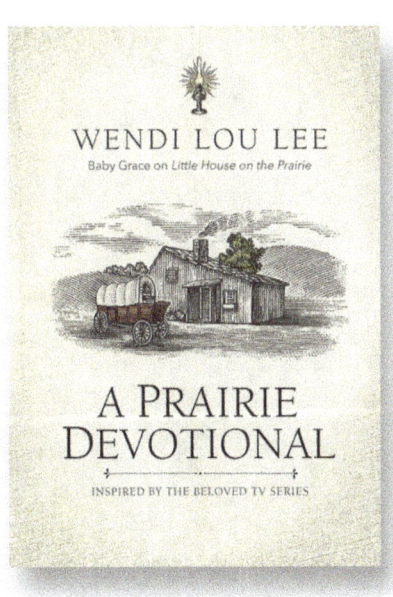